# First Things First

## An Illustrated Collection of Sayings
## Useful and Familiar for Children

### BETTY FRASER

HarperCollins*Publishers*

5437181

First Things First
Designed by Andrew Rhodes

Library of Congress Cataloging-in-Publication Data
Fraser, Betty.
  First things first.

  Summary: An illustrated collection of familiar proverbs with
suggestions for their proper use.
  1. Proverbs, American.   2. Proverbs, English.   [1. Proverbs.]
I. Title.
PN6429.F73   1990          398'.921               86-42993
ISBN 0-06-021854-1
ISBN 0-06-021855-X (lib. bdg.)
ISBN 0-06-443300-5 (pbk.)

# First Things First

An Illustrated Collection of Sayings
Useful and Familiar for Children

# What to say when you are the first

# What to say when you are the last

# What to say when you are tired of hearing someone talk about it

# What to say when everyone is bossy and nothing gets done right

Too many cooks spoil the broth

# What to say when everyone helps

Many hands make light work

# What to say when you find something you would like to keep

Honesty
is the
best policy

# What to say
# when you can't do it the first time

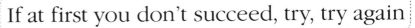

If at first you don't succeed, try, try again

# What to say
# when you see people doing the same things

# What to say
# when you had to find out for yourself

Experience
is the best teacher

# What to do when you don't know what to say

# What to say when it seems as though what someone else has is better

# What to say when things go badly

Every cloud has a silver lining

# What to say when you didn't believe it

Seeing is believing

Seeing is believing

Seeing is believing

# What to say
# when it isn't what you thought it would be

# What to say when you need help

# What to say when you pay someone back

# What to say
# when you feel brave and ready to do it

# What to say
# when you aren't ready

Better safe than sorry

One step at a time

# What to say when someone is going too fast

# What to say when someone is going too slow

# What to say
# when you spill it, drop it, or break it

# What to do when you don't know what to do

Do unto others as you would have them do unto you

# What to say when it's all done

All good things must come to an end